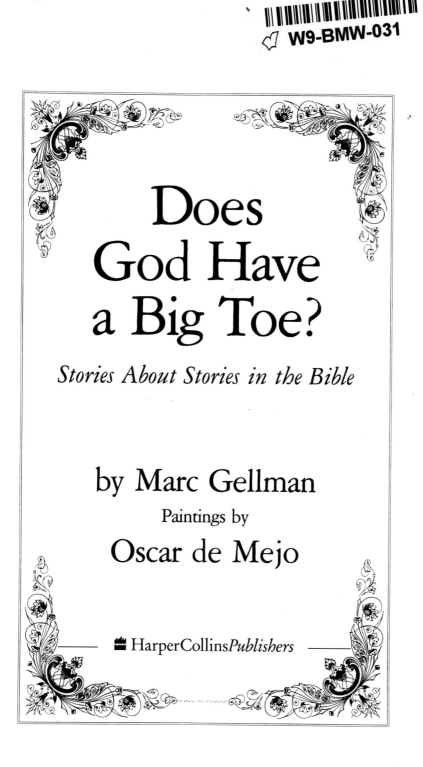

Does God Have a Big Toe?

Stories About Stories in the Bible

by Marc Gellman

Paintings by

Oscar de Mejo

HarperCollins*Publishers*

Does God Have a Big Toe?
Stories About Stories in the Bible

Library of Congress Cataloging-in-Publication Data
Gellman, Marc
    Does God have a big toe? : stories about stories in the Bible /
by Marc Gellman ; paintings by Oscar de Mejo.
        p.   cm.
    Summary: A collection of humorous stories derived from Bible
stories in the Old Testament.
    ISBN 0-06-022432-0. — ISBN 0-06-022433-9 (lib. bdg.)
    ISBN 0-06-440453-6 (pbk.)
    [1. Humorous Stories.]   I. De Mejo, Oscar, ill.   II. Title.
PZ7.G28355Do   1989   89-1893
[Fic]—dc19   CIP
                                                        AC

My Thanks

Many of these stories appeared in earlier versions over the last ten years in *Moment* magazine. I'd like to thank Leibel Fein, the former editor of *Moment*, for all his years of support and encouragement, and all the readers of *Moment*, who have been so generous. I'd also like to thank my editor, Laura Geringer, for falling in love with these stories. Her advice was always gentle and wise.

I believe the best way to pray is to sing and the best way to tell a story is to paint a picture. I cannot sing or paint, but I have been blessed with Oscar de Mejo's visual interpretations of the stories I had no choice but to put into words.

I'd like to thank my wife, Betty, for her sustaining love, and our children, Mara and Max, to whom I dedicate this book. They are almost grown but they were babies when I first began to write these stories for them. I wanted Mara and Max to have something that they could read and that they could read to their children and be able to say, "Look, this was how our father loved the Bible."

God bless you all.

Contents

I:
—— ADAM'S ANIMALS ——

II:
DOES GOD HAVE
—— A BIG TOE? ——

AUTHOR'S NOTE

One way to understand a story is to have someone explain it to you. They will probably say, "Listen to me, this is what that story means . . ." and then they will tell you something. That is one way to understand the Bible, but I don't think it's a very good way. The person who explains the story might be wrong and, in any event, explaining stories from the Bible only makes sense if there is just one right way to understand that story. But the stories in the Bible are so rich and deep and packed with a thousand different meanings that they cannot be explained just one right way. The best way to understand a story in the Bible is to make up another story about it. And that is what I have done in this book.

In this book I have written new stories about the old stories in the Bible. Each of my stories is a way of understanding the Bible stories a little better. Each of my stories is a way of trying to answer some question about that story in the Bible, but I never really tell you what question I am trying to answer. That would be too much like an explanation.

Jews and Christians and Moslems have been writing stories about stories in the Bible for a very long time. I am a Jew and I am a rabbi. In my tradition the people who write stories about stories in the Bible are called *darshanim*, and the stories they write about the stories in the Bible are called *midrashim*. A *midrash* is the Jewish name for a story about a story in the Bible. There are collections of old *midrashim* written by old rabbis and *darshanim*, and I have learned from them, but the stories in this book are new. They are modern *midrashim*.

I am not exactly sure of all the ways they are different and all the ways they are the same as the old *midrashim*. It doesn't matter. What matters is that it's a way that the love of the Bible shines forth and lifts up children and their parents and whispers to them, "Listen to the words of the Bible! Listen to them with your ears and your heart and your mind and your soul."

Before there was anything, there was God, a few angels, and a huge swirling glob of rocks and water with no place to go. The angels asked God, "Why don't you clean up this mess?"

So God collected rocks from the huge swirling glob and put them together in clumps and said, "Some of these clumps of rocks will be planets, and some will be stars, and some of these rocks will be . . . just rocks."

Then God collected water from the huge swirling glob and put it together in pools of water and said, "Some of these pools of water will be oceans, and some will become clouds, and some of this water will be . . . just water."

Then the angels said, "Well God, it's neater now, but is it finished?" And God answered . . .

"NOPE!"

On some of the rocks God placed growing things, and creeping things, and things that only God knows what they are, and when God had done all this, the

angels asked God, "Is the world finished now?" And God answered:

"NOPE!"

God made a man and a woman from some of the water and dust and said to them, "I am tired now. Please finish up the world for me . . . really it's almost done." But the man and woman said, "We can't finish the world alone! You have the plans and we are too little."

"You are big enough," God answered them. "But I agree to this. If you keep trying to finish the world, I will be your partner."

The man and the woman asked, "What's a partner?" and God answered, "A partner is someone you work with on a big thing that neither of you can do alone. If you have a partner, it means that you can never give up, because your partner is depending on you. On the days you think I am not doing enough and on the days I think you are not doing enough, even on those days we are still partners and we must not stop trying to finish the world. That's the deal." And they all agreed to that deal.

Then the angels asked God, "Is the world finished yet?" and God answered, "I don't know. Go ask my partners."

ADAM'S ANIMALS

Adam's Animals

God made and named almost everything in the world. God made and named Heaven. God made and named Earth. God made and named the sun and the moon, the stars and the waters. God made and named almost everything. God even made and named the first man, "Adam," which means "red earth" because God made the first man out of red earth.

But God did not name the animals.

God thought, "I want Adam and Adam's children to protect and care for these animals. Maybe if I let Adam name the animals, he will get to know them better and really take care of them."

Well, when Adam heard that he could name the animals, he was so happy. He ran right over to a brown furry with teeth who was sleeping under a tree and yelled in its ear, "I AM GOING TO NAME YOU!"

The brown furry with teeth opened one eye, yawned, and went back to sleep.

Very soon, Adam realized he didn't know what to name the brown furry with teeth, or, for that matter, any of the other animals. Adam sat down on the sleeping brown furry with teeth to think up a plan for naming the animals. Suddenly it came to him: "I know! I will give each animal a number. That way, when I want to call an animal I can just call its number." Adam looked down at the brown furry with teeth, lifted up its ear, and screamed, "YOU ARE NUMBER ONE!"

The brown furry opened one eye, yawned, and went back to sleep.

Adam spent the rest of that day numbering the animals. He gave numbers to slimy swimmers with no fins, fuzzy hoppers with twitchy noses, squeaky flyers with colored feathers, chirping swingers with curling tails, speedy crawlers with tiny feet, scaly swimmers with red eyes, and a whole bunch of gray, black, and white furries with teeth who looked like they were related to Number One. In the late afternoon, somewhere between the numbering of the tiny sand-diggers and the swarming wood-eaters, Adam lost count! He plopped down again on the brown furry with teeth to think up a new plan for naming the animals.

After a time, Adam decided, "I will call all the animals 'Hey You!' That way, when I need an animal

I will only have to remember one name." The next day, Adam needed a big rock moved out of his way. He wanted the large - gray - wrinkled - up - long - nosed - big - eared - white - tusked - tree - eating - stomper for the job, so he yelled out, "HEY YOU! Come over here and move this rock!" But instead of the large - gray - wrinkled - up - long - nosed - big - eared - white - tusked - tree - eating - stomper, a rather - small - quite - noisy - banana - eating - chirping - swinger hopped on top of the rock and began eating a banana. Adam was quite discouraged and returned to the brown furry with teeth to think up a new plan for naming the animals, but this time nothing came to him.

Then the brown furry woke up, shook Adam into a nearby bush, growled a huge growl, looked Adam in the eye, and said to him, "Listen to me! With all your talking you never once thought to ask us—the animals—what we would like to be named. Why don't you try that? Now, I don't know what they call a skinny-hairless-red-earth-foot-walker like you, but they call me a *bear*!"

So Adam asked all the animals what they wanted to be called. And you know what? They told him!

The First New Year

When Adam was first put into the Garden of Eden, he was amazed at everything. The smell of the flowers made him dance. The sound of the birds made him sing for joy. But of all the things that amazed Adam in the Garden of Eden, by far the most amazing thing was the sun. The sun was so far away he could not touch it, and yet it warmed his face as if it were close.

Imagine Adam's surprise when the sun sank right down behind the edge of the garden and disappeared! Adam did not notice the sinking of the sun until it had already sunk, and then everything turned dark and cold. Adam was afraid, and so were the animals! They all crowded around him and he tried to look brave. But none of them looked very brave, shivering through that first cold night.

After a while Adam fell asleep, but later he was awakened by a warm feeling on the back of his neck. He whirled around and saw the sun peeking over the other side of the garden! Adam did not understand how the sun was able to sneak around and come up on the other side of the Garden of Eden. But he was happy that the sun was in the sky again and he was not cold.

Adam tried to reassure all the animals that the sun was back to stay, but after some time they came rushing over to Adam. "It's sinking again!" they cried. And sure enough, the sun was sinking lower and lower in the sky. "Let's build something to stop the sun from sinking," they said. So the animals scurried around piling stuff at just the spot where the sun sank. They hoped that the sun would hit their pile of junk and stop at the edge of the Garden of Eden just before it sank and everything got cold again.

The monkey piled bananas and the elephant piled tree trunks and the squirrel piled nuts and the pile of stuff rose high over the wall that surrounded the Garden of Eden. But then the sun just sank right behind all that stuff, and it was dark again and cold again and the animals were frightened again—and so was Adam.

Then God explained to Adam that the sun would sink again and again and again, and that there was nothing he or the animals could do to stop it. But God also said that there was nothing to worry about because in a few hours the sun would rise again over the other side of the garden.

God explained to Adam that separating the sinking and rising and sinking of the sun was something called "time." And God explained to Adam that the time from one sun sinking to another sun sinking was one day, the time of seven sun sinkings was one week, and the time of four weeks of sun sinkings was one month, and the time of twelve months was one year. "Do you understand?" God asked Adam. "Sure," said Adam, who actually had no idea what God was talking about.

What Adam thought was this, "After one day I'm all right because I still have six others before the week is over. After the week is over I'm okay because I still have three other weeks before the month is over. And then I have eleven other months to use up." So Adam went on about his work in the Garden of Eden.

Days and weeks and months went by and Adam marked them all but did not think much of it, until one day Adam noticed that eleven months and three weeks and six days had been used up. Then it hit him, "I have used up all the time! What am I going to do now? Tonight the sun will sink and it will never rise again because this is the end of time. I am going to have to wander around in the dark, and it is going to be cold all the time and I am going to trip over things. O Lord, what will I do now?"

On that last day of the last week of the last month of the year, Adam said good-bye to the animals of the Garden of Eden. He called them together near the big tree in the middle of the garden and said, "I don't know if I will see you tomorrow because I don't know if there is going to be a tomorrow. Before the sun sinks for the last time, I wanted you all to know that you were good friends. If I did anything to hurt you in any way, I'm sorry and I hope you will forgive me."

The animals hugged Adam and each other and bunched up together because they figured that they would soon be cold, and they cried a little as they watched the sun sink for the last time behind the edge of the garden. Then . . . after a while . . . the sun peeped up over the other side of the garden just as it had every morning of the first year. A new day had begun. It was the first day of the second year!

Then Adam heard God counting, "Ten years is one decade . . . ten decades is one century . . . ten centuries is one millennium . . . ten millennia is . . ." but by this time Adam had fallen asleep.

When Adam woke up, he smelled the flowers, heard the birds singing, and thanked God for making time way big enough.

The Man Who Loved a Tree

Adam was the only person ever in the whole wide world who never had a mom or a dad. When you are the first person, nobody came before you. That's what it means to be the first person. But being the first person caused some big problems for Adam and for God. Adam had nobody to feed him. So God made Adam old enough to feed himself. Adam had nobody to teach him. So God made Adam smart enough to teach himself. Adam had nobody to kiss him. But God did not know how to solve that problem right away.

Very soon Adam turned lonely, and before God could figure out what to do, Adam took a liking to a big old fruit tree in the middle of the Garden of Eden. Of course that big old tree didn't say a word to Adam, but Adam spoke to the tree as if it were his best friend. He would say: "Hiya, tree! How ya doin', tree! Great day today, tree! Want a drink of water, tree?"

Adam sat in the shade of the tree during the heat

of the day. He slept curled up around the tree every night. He would listen for hours to the sound of wind rustling through its leaves.

God was not happy about Adam's friendship with the tree. God wanted Adam to pick a living-breathing - moving - around - pal, not a stuck - in - the - mud - covered - with - bark - and - bugs - pal. So God hurried and made Eve, and brought Eve to Adam expecting of course that they would become best friends right away. Adam liked Eve, but he liked the tree better. In fact, Adam loved that tree.

"Eve is too soft. She doesn't have any bark, or leaves, or fruit," he thought.

Eve did her best to get Adam to love her. She would put leaves in her hair, twigs in her ears, and fruit in her nose all to make herself more beautiful in Adam's eyes. But Adam still loved the tree.

God tried to help Eve by telling Adam that he could not eat any more fruit from that tree. But that did not help. Adam would sit under the tree looking up at the fruit and sighing.

Eve decided that God was not going to solve her problem. So she went to the snake, who told her to eat the fruit from the tree and give some to Adam and then everything would be all right.

The next day when Adam woke up, there was Eve, sitting next to him and holding some of the forbidden fruit she had picked from the tree. Adam couldn't believe it. "Don't you know God told us not to eat that fruit?"

But Eve said, "I wanted you to have it because I know how much you love this tree."

"You did this for me?" Adam asked. Eve nodded and Adam hugged her and together they ate the fruit.

God was happy to get Adam and Eve out of the Garden of Eden and away from that tree. Outside the garden Adam and Eve slept curled around each other, and they kissed. To shade them from the hot sun, Adam planted a fruit tree.

He liked the new tree a lot, but he loved Eve.

No Lists on the Sabbath!

I know you wish you could have lived in the Garden of Eden. I know. Great weather, no problems, good food, and water that doesn't taste funny. But believe me when I tell you that the Garden of Eden was no piece of cake, because Adam lived there, and Adam was a list maker. In fact, Adam was the worst list maker of all time.

The elephant woke up one morning to find his trunk stuck through a huge leaf on which Adam had written in berry ink,

Elephant list for today:
1. Dump all the broken branches outside the garden.
2. Hose down the dirty dishes.
3. Squash some coconuts for lunch.

The monkey woke up one morning to find a banana peel tied around its tail on which Adam had written in berry ink,

Monkey list for today:
1. Dump the rotten fruit outside the garden.
2. Pick bananas for supper.
3. Don't eat the bananas you pick for supper.

Come morning, almost every animal woke up with a list, and all day long Adam would scurry around checking up on the animals and pestering them to see how they were coming with their lists.

One day, the animals got together and said to God, "This guy Adam is such a pest! Can't you move us out of here? Or better yet, can't you move him out of here?"

God said, "Wait for the Sabbath. There are no lists on the Sabbath."

On the morning of the seventh day Adam woke up bright and early to make his lists. He went to get his berry ink pot to write out a list for the elephant, but the ink was dry.

"No problem," said Adam. "I will just go out and pick some more berries for the inkwell." But when Adam came to the berry patch, all the berries were gone.

"I bet this is the work of the monkey," Adam complained. "But not to worry, I will scratch out my lists for all the animals in the sand on the beach."

Adam took a stick and started writing lists in the

wet sand. But a wave came along and erased all the lists. Adam thought this was very strange, because the Garden of Eden was near a river. He had never before seen a wave that big in the river.

So Adam sat down to rest. And he felt good just resting. Then the monkey came by. "No lists on the Sabbath!" he chirped.

The elephant came by and trumpeted, "No lists on the Sabbath!"

And the animals all wished Adam a good day of rest.

The Tomato Plant

The Garden of Eden had everything. Bears and monkeys, fish and butterflies—everything. Even the first man and woman, Adam and Eve, were there. Nothing ever died in the garden, so of course nothing was ever born to replace it. The Garden of Eden had everything, but everything was always just the same.

One day Adam and Eve came upon a crack in the big wall that surrounded the garden. Looking through the crack, they saw that in the brown dust outside the garden a tomato plant was growing. At first they could hardly recognize it. In the garden, all the tomato plants were tall and full and green with many big red tomatoes on each stem. What they saw through the crack in the wall was a puny and shriveled up little thing with just one tiny green tomato barely hanging on to one of the stems.

Every day Adam and Eve would come to the crack and peep through to see how the only thing growing outside the Garden of Eden was doing. One day the little tomato plant drooped over and turned brown.

Adam looked at Eve and said, "It never looked good, but now it looks worse."

Eve looked at Adam and said, "Whatever could have happened to it?"

They sat there for a long time, peeping through the crack in the wall at the little tomato plant that had drooped over and turned brown.

After a long while, God spoke to them saying, "The tomato plant is dead." Adam and Eve cried. They asked God, "Why did it have to die? Nothing dies here in the garden." But God would not answer this question no matter how many times they asked.

So they became angry at God. They demanded that God let them out of the Garden of Eden so they could take care of the tomato plant. God said to them, "You can leave, but you can't come back."

Well, Adam and Eve got up and walked right out of the garden and right over to the little tomato plant that had drooped over and turned brown. Inside the garden nothing needed help, and even though outside the garden everything needed help, they were not sorry that they could not return.

Adam picked up the tiny green tomato and Eve planted it in the brown dust. For many days they watered the ground, kept the weeds away, and waited.

Then it happened! A green shoot poked up through the dusty ground, and in a few days it became . . . a tomato plant! Full and green with many big red tomatoes on each stem!

In the days that followed, when the man and the woman looked at the strong new tomato plant, they would also think of the scraggly little plant they had once peeked at through the crack in the wall. It was a funny feeling. They were happy and sad at the very same time.

Water All Around

When God first made the world, nothing turned out right, so God decided to start all over again. When the animals heard about this, they were frightened. They decided to ask God not to end the world. But none of them knew where God lived, so they all flew and flopped, rolled and ran, jerked and jumped, crept and crawled, slithered and slid to the different places they thought God lived.

The elephant said, "I am the biggest animal, but God must be bigger than I. Surely I will find God in the biggest thing."

The elephant came to a mountain. "This is the biggest thing around, so it must be God!" And the elephant asked the mountain not to end the world.

The eagle said, "I can fly higher than any animal, but God must fly higher than I. Surely I will find God in the highest thing." The eagle flew higher and higher—far higher than any bird had ever flown before.

The eagle saw a fluffy white cloud that was even higher than he. "This is the highest thing, so it must be God." And the eagle asked the cloud not to end the world.

The lion said, "My roar is the loudest animal sound, but God must be louder than I. Surely I will find God in the loudest thing!" So the lion roared and roared and roared and roared.

Suddenly the clouds gathered together, turned black, and sent out thunder and lightning. "This is the loudest thing, so it must be God." And the lion asked the thunder not to end the world.

Soon the elephant realized that the mountain wasn't God because it didn't answer him.

Soon the eagle realized that the cloud wasn't God because it blew away.

Soon the lion realized that the thunder wasn't God because it stopped.

Soon all the animals were yelling, "We have to find God or we're done for!"

Then the fish spoke up. "In the oceans and seas and rivers and lakes where we live, water is everywhere. There is water above and water below. There is water all around. If the water is everywhere, God must be everywhere too."

When God heard what the fish said, the whole

world shone and the black clouds blew away. Then God said to the animals, "When I end the world, I will save two of each kind of animal so that when the world starts over, you can start over too. But as for the fish . . . I will save *all* of them, because only they knew where to find God."

Noah's Friends

Like most people, Noah ignored bad news. For example, when God told Noah that only his family would be saved from the big flood, Noah figured, "God is very busy. Maybe the rest of the passenger list is in the mail. After all, this ark God wants me to build is huge. I'm sure there will be more than enough room for *all* my friends."

Later on, when God told Noah to take pairs of all the animals onto the ark, Noah understood right then that there would be no room for his friends.

Noah didn't have the heart to come right out and tell his friends. But he did try to tell them in a roundabout way. He said to his pal Jabal, "You know Jabal, this might be a very good time for you to take those swimming lessons you have been talking about for so long."

And to his friend Jehaz, "Jehaz, ol' buddy, take my advice and move your house to the top of that very high mountain. The view is great over there, and it's much cooler in the summertime." But Noah just could not bear to come right out and tell his friends about the flood.

Noah's friends didn't pay much attention to his advice. But they became very curious about the huge pile of wood in Noah's front yard. Noah told them it was just a statue. And even after the thing really looked like a boat, he said it was just a statue of a boat.

Noah's friends thought he was nuts. But then they thought that Noah was nuts even before he started building the ark.

Then the animals started to arrive. Noah still could not tell his friends the truth. So he said the animals were just there to pull the boat to the sea. But his friends did not believe him.

"Chipmunks?" asked one.

"Rabbits?" asked another. And they shook their heads.

On the day the rains began, the animals all ran into the ark. The water began to cover the ground. And Noah's friends ran to the ark, banged on the door, and called up to Noah, who was peeping over the side of the ark: "Hey Noah, you rat, let us in! We're your *friends*! You can't float off and leave us here to drown. Save us, Noah! Save us!"

Noah looked down with tears in his eyes and said, "I didn't pick me. God picked me. What can I do?"

Noah's friends Jehaz and Jabal came to the ark dressed in a zebra suit. They demanded to be let in. Noah knew it was them. They were too lumpy to be a zebra. "Let us—I mean, let me in," they said. "You forgot me when you gathered in all the animals. I am a Jehaz—I mean—a zebra." Noah looked down on his friends and spoke through his tears.

"My dear friends, I don't know how I can live without you. The world was not this bad when God gave it to us. I don't know why God is saving me. Maybe God needs somebody to tell the story of how we all messed up the world. Maybe God wants some of the old life to grow up in a new clean place. Honestly, I don't know. All I know is that I didn't pick me. God picked me. I will remember you always. And I will tell the story of how to live in the right way. The story we all were told by God and by our parents but that we forgot. Maybe my children's children will learn the story. And then maybe the world will not turn bad again. And then nobody will ever have to say good-bye to his friends again. I love you. I am sorry for you, sorry for the animals, sorry for me, and sorry for God."

Then the great rains came and flooded all the earth.

Some say it was just rain, but others say that it was God's tears.

The Bird-Feather Rainbow

From the beginning, God knew that people would try to act like they were better than their neighbors. But honestly, God never expected to have the same problem with the animals. As soon as they were created, they started to argue about who had the most beautiful hooves, hair, fur, scales, fangs, or feathers. And the worst of the bunch by far were the birds.

When the time came for Noah to round up all the animals for the ark, he almost gave up when he had to settle the birds in their nesting places. The best nesting spot was on the great wooden beam that ran across the ark. And the best place on that beam was right next to the only window on the ark. It was grabbed right away by the parrots, who would only allow the bright-pink flamingos to nest next to them, who would only allow the canaries next to them, who would only allow the cardinals next to them, who would only allow the blue jays next to them, and so on right down the beam.

At the farthest, darkest end of the bird beam nested the raven and the dove. Their feathers were just plain black and just plain white, so no other birds would have anything to do with them.

After one hundred and fifty days and nights in the ark everyone was going crazy. Suddenly, *thud! crunch!* the ark stopped rocking in the waves and came to rest. With a loud growling, hissing, mooing, croaking, squeaking, and cawing, the animals said, *"Let us out of here!"*

But when Noah opened the window, a cold blast of wind howled in from the black sky. All the animals turned to their neighbors and said, "You first."

Noah decided that a bird should go out and explore. So he asked the parrot next to the window, but the parrot just ruffled her feathers and squawked, "Don't be ridiculous! My feathers are much too beautiful to be messed up in that awful wind. Send the flamingo." The flamingo then stood up and sneered, "It's much too cold out there for me. Send the canary." And so it went, right down the bird beam with all the birds chirping the reasons why they could not fly outside the ark until with a *caw!* and a *whoosh!* the raven flew out the window and into the cold windy night.

When the raven did not return after several days, Noah asked the birds if one of them would go out and try to find the raven. But all the birds found new reasons why they could not go. All except the dove, that is, who whooshed out the window to try and find her friend the raven in the black and windy sky.

After a long flight, the dove found the raven perched in an olive tree on a tiny island in the great flood sea. After munching on a few fresh olives, the dove said, "Let's go back and tell our friends the birds that there is land out here."

"Our *friends?*" laughed the raven. "Those birds don't care if we ever return. Why don't you just stay here with me, and no bird with colored feathers will ever make fun of us again."

But the dove said, "I don't think it's fair for us to sit here munching olives while everyone else is cooped up in the ark." And off she flew.

Meanwhile, back at the ark, Noah stood at the little window, staring out into the cold night for some sign of either the raven or the dove. The parrot kept pestering Noah: "Close the window! They're lost. We're cold. And you're crazy!" But Noah continued to stand at the open window, looking, listening, freezing, and sneezing.

The dove was lost. Her white wings were dipping closer and closer to the churning black waves, and she felt that she could not flap her tired wings another flap. Then, through the roaring wind, the dove heard a *ha-choo!* Following the sound, she came to Noah's outstretched hand, and he brought her into the warm ark.

When the dove reported that there was land out there, none of the birds believed her. The next morning, when they woke up, the dove was gone. Her little nest at the end of the bird beam was soaked with tears.

"I knew they wouldn't believe you," said the raven to the dove when she returned to the olive tree, which was now on the top of a hill on a large island in the great flood sea. "Stay with me and forget about them. Here, have an olive."

"I don't want an olive, but I will take an olive leaf," said the dove. "This will show them that there really *is* land out here."

"Won't you ever learn?" said the raven. "They're too scared to leave the ark."

"And you, my friend, are too scared to leave this island and live with them," said the dove as she flew off, a white speck against a black sky.

Soon the dove was lost at sea and straining her ears for Noah's *ha-choo* or a flicker of light from the ark. But all the dove heard was wind and waves, wind and waves.

Then suddenly, up ahead, the dove saw something

very strange. Rising out of the sea was a rainbow! Flying closer she saw that the rainbow was fluttering in the wind. And it was chirping!

In fact, the beautiful rainbow was a tower of birds flapping their wings against the strong wind. The parrot was flying up and down the bird-feather rainbow, squawking orders: "Stay in line, you flamingos! Watch out for the hummingbirds, you blue jays! Remember, our friend Noah is sick with a cold. And our friend the dove is lost at sea, just because we were too dumb to believe her. So—budgie birds, flap those wings!"

When the two great doors of the ark swung open and all the animals were let out at last, they were greeted by a wondrous sight. A real rainbow was shining in the sky, stretching from the ark at one end to an olive tree on top of a mountain at the other.

That night, before all the birds flew off to their new homes in the new world, they nested together in the olive tree. And on the very top branch were the raven and the dove.

The dove fell asleep quickly. But the raven busied himself by passing out olives to all his new friends with colored feathers.

In the morning the birds were gone. But the rainbow remained.

DOES
GOD HAVE
A BIG TOE?

Does God Have a Big Toe?

Long ago, all the people lived in one place called "Babel." Not only did every person live in the same place, but every person spoke the same language. All of which made life very easy. Getting the news was easy, and you didn't have to learn a new language in high school.

But Arinna's question changed all that.

Arinna asked: "Mommy, I have a big toe, and you have a big toe, and Daddy has a big toe. Does God have a big toe too?"

Now everything might have been all right if Arinna's mother had just said, "Arinna, God is not a person. God is special and invisible and wonderful and God is the creator of the universe. God has made each of us in God's image. But God is not a person. And that is why God does not have a big toe." But Arinna's mother was busy with something and said, "Go ask your father."

So she did, but Arinna's father was also busy with

something, and he told her, "Go ask your grandpa." So she did.

Grandpa was in his garden, digging up weeds with his pal Fred, who worked in the king's palace. Arinna asked, "Grandpa, I have a big toe and Mommy has a big toe and Daddy has a big toe and you have a big toe and Fred has a big toe. Does God have a big toe too?"

Now Arinna's grandpa was old and a little hard of hearing, and he said, "Does God have a big hoe? Why I don't know if God has a big hoe. I suppose if God has a garden, then God must have a hoe. After all, you can't get rid of weeds without a hoe." Fred whispered to Arinna that he would ask the king the next day at work.

The king thought and thought and then issued a proclamation:

"You, the people of Babel, will build a tower up to the sky so that I, your king, can stand on top of this tower and look at God's foot. Then I will tell you if God has a big toe."

The king ordered the builders to use only the best bricks and the best tar to stick them together. The Tower of Babel grew higher and higher every day.

Now God knew that if everybody was working on the tower, then nobody would work in the fields

growing things. Nobody would be in the shops making things. God knew that soon all the bricks and
tar in Babel would be used up. And the people of
Babel would have nothing left to build houses.

God thought about just knocking down the tower,
but God knew for sure that the Babelians would just
build it up again to see if God had a big toe. There
was only one thing to do.

The next day, when Arinna came to watch the
work on the tower, she heard Fred ask his friend
for a brick, and his friend answered *"Mah atah
rotzeh?"* and turned to another guy with tar, who
said, *"Arigato,"* and asked a guy with a shovel, who
said, *"Como está?"* and looked at a fellow with a
wheelbarrow, who said *"Gesundheit."*

Soon bricks and tar were flying everywhere, and
by the end of the day people who spoke the same
language were heading out of town together.

Arinna and her family decided to leave town
too—with Fred, Grandpa, and a few other people
they could still understand. They packed up everything they owned and left Babel.

On the cart, Arinna was quiet for a while and then
asked: "Mommy, I have a belly button, and you have
a belly button, and Daddy has a belly button. Does
God have a belly button too?"

Most people do not realize it, but God put in calls to other people before finally putting in a call to Abram.

First God called Eber and said, "Eber, leave your country and your neighbors and your family and go to a land I will show to you, and I will make of you a great nation and I will bless you and make your name great and you will be a blessing; all who bless you will be blessed and all who curse you will be cursed and through you all the nations of the earth shall be blessed."

And Eber said, "Who are you?" And God said, "God." And Eber said, "The god of what?" And God said, "The God of everything." And Eber said, "Don't be ridiculous, there is no god of everything. There is a god of the sun and a god of the moon, a god of the night and a god of the day, a god of the mountains and a god of the valleys, a god of the forests and a god of the deserts. If you ask me, you are a little late. Everything already has a god, and there is no god of everything. Maybe if you look hard, you can find something that doesn't already have a god. As a matter of fact, I think there is no god of frogs at the moment. Why don't you go check that out and then we can talk, because there just is no god of everything."

But Eber and God never talked again.

The next person God called was Peleg. God said, "Peleg, leave your country and your neighbors and your family and go to a land I will show to you, and I will make of you a great nation and I will bless you and make your name great and you will be a blessing; all who bless you will be blessed and all who curse you will be cursed and through you all the nations of the earth shall be blessed."

And Peleg said, "Who are you?" And God said, "God." And Peleg said, "Where are you?" And God said, "I am everywhere." And Peleg said, "If you are everywhere where do they put your statue so that people can bow down to you?" And God said, "I am invisible and no one may make a statue of me." Peleg rolled on the ground with laughter. "Now let me get this straight! You are the invisible god of everything with no statue, and you want me to leave my home and follow you to a place you will show me? Do you think I am crazy? Now look, why don't

· 48 ·

you go to a good idol maker and have a nice sculpture made of your image, and then we can find a nice place to put it down where people can bow to it, and then we can talk."

But God and Peleg never talked again.

Then God went to Serug and said, "Serug, leave your country and your neighbors and your family and go to a land I will show to you, and I will make of you a great nation and I will bless you and make your name great and you will be a blessing; all who bless you will be blessed and all who curse you will be cursed and through you all the nations of the earth shall be blessed."

And Serug said, "Who are you?" And God said, "God." And Serug said, "What will you give *me?*" And God said, "I just told you." And Serug said, "You don't understand. I am not interested in moving anywhere or doing anything just so that my great-great-great-grandchildren will be a great nation. I want to know what is in this deal for me right now. Maybe if you showered me with some of those blessings up front I might be convinced. How about giving me all the money in the world and the kingship of all the lands? What do you say?"

But God said nothing. Then Serug said, "All right, let's be reasonable. I will go wherever you want for *most* of the money in the world and the kingship of the five largest countries. How about that?" But God said nothing.

That was the last Serug ever heard from God.

By that time, God was not sure about finding the right man. But God went to Abram and said, "Abram, leave your country and your neighbors and your family and go to a land I will show to you, and I will make of you a great nation and I will bless you and make your name great and you will be a blessing; all who bless you will be blessed and all who curse you will be cursed and through you all the nations of the earth shall be blessed."

And Abram said, "I will go, but there is just one thing I want." God asked what that one thing was, and Abram answered, "I want to take my family with me."

God asked him, "That's it? You just want your family to come with you? Don't you want to see me?" And Abram said, "No." And God asked, "Don't you want to bow down to a statue of me?" And Abram said, "No." And God asked, "Abram, don't you want anything for yourself?" And Abram said, "No."

Right then God decided not to ask any more questions, and God let Abram gather his family and pack their things for the journey to the place that God would show to them.

Right then God knew that the right man was going to the right place at the right time for the right reasons. God also knew that such things hardly ever happen.

Rebekah
and the Camel
Who Made No Noise

Abram, whom God renamed Abraham, told Eliezer his servant to go back east to find a wife for his son Isaac. Eliezer did not want to go. But Abraham told him that God would help out by sending along an angel. Abraham had no idea at the time how God would do this, and frankly, neither did God.

Now, Eliezer wasn't an angel. And the other servants weren't angels. So that just left the camels. God figured he would make one of the camels into an angel just for the trip. After all, the point of the journey was to find a wife for Isaac. And to do this Eliezer and the angel had to watch the women of the east without being noticed. God figured that if Eliezer took along a guy with wings, white robes, a halo, and a harp who floated through the air, they might be noticed. So that is why the angel had to be a camel.

When God asked for volunteers, nobody raised a wing. So God called upon Max. Max was the angel God called upon for all the really tough jobs. Max was the one who had to tell the extra lions and tigers that they could not go on the ark with Noah. Max was the angel who had to kick the snake out of the Garden of Eden. Max was the angel who had to collect all the slimy bugs for Adam to name. Max got all the tough jobs.

So the caravan to the east finally took off with Eliezer riding on Max. Max found that speaking camel was a cinch, but making the other camel noises was not so easy. Also, one of the girl camels liked Max and kept licking his nose.

Now Rebekah, the granddaughter of Abraham's brother Nahor, was sweet, kind, and beautiful. And she loved animals. People in the town said that Rebekah could speak the languages of chipmunks and rabbits, lizards and snakes, elephants and mice, eagles and goats. But Rebekah did not like camels.

It was not the fact that they were ugly. It was not the fact that they drank so much water that she had to go to the well a hundred times to fill their humps. What bothered Rebekah most was the loud camel noises they made.

One day Eliezer and his caravan of ten camels (really it was nine camels and a Max) came to the well of the city where Nahor lived. They arrived late in the afternoon. The women of the city were out drawing water for the flocks of sheep and goats. There were not many camels in the city where Nahor lived, because the people didn't travel much. Also, they had a small well and worried that too many camels would drink up all the water.

When the women saw Eliezer and his camel caravan, they shooed them away: "Go! Get out of here! Find another well!" Eliezer started to leave, but the camels sat down and started to make every noise they could. Rebekah came over to Eliezer and said in front of all the women, "You may drink from our well. And your camels may drink too."

Then Rebekah walked over to Max and looked at him in a funny way. She spoke to him in camel, saying, "You are very sweet. You did not complain and you don't make camel noises. Come, you shall be the first to drink."

Max answered her in camel, "My humps are still full. Water the other camels first."

So Rebekah led the camels to the well and they drank and Eliezer drank, and finally Max drank. Rebekah worked most of the day drawing water for all the flocks and the camels. In the morning, Eliezer asked Rebekah to return with him to become Isaac's wife. She said, "Yes."

So the caravan of Eliezer came to the city of Nahor

with ten camels, but left with only nine. Rebekah looked all over for the quiet camel who did not make camel noises. But she could not find him.

Up in Heaven, Max was climbing out of his camel suit. God kissed Max in the way that God kisses angels, and thanked him. Then God said, "Max, in a little while I am going to need an angel to speak to Moses out of a burning bush. There is a fireproof suit over there in the corner. Why don't you just try it on for size?"

The Strong Man Who Cried

Jacob cried a lot. Jacob cried when he was happy. Jacob cried when he was sad. But mostly Jacob cried when he saw beautiful things. The sight of a fresh new flower or a sunset would fill him with happiness and he would just cry. He couldn't help it. But his father Isaac was not happy about having a son who cried a lot.

Isaac would not take Jacob hunting because Jacob would cry at the thought of some furry little animal becoming his supper. So Isaac would take his other son Esau, who loved to hunt and never cried.

"Why can't you be more like your brother Esau?" Isaac would scold Jacob. "He hunts and fights and never cries. He is a real man."

And Jacob would answer, "I cry when I feel like crying. I just can't change that." Then Isaac would stomp off, kick the dirt, and mutter strange words.

Meanwhile, Rachel, who was Jacob's cousin living in a place called Harran, was also having trouble with her father. Rachel was a shepherd, and this drove her father Laban crazy. Day and night he would yell at her, "Get away from those sheep and goats! Why can't you be more like your sister Leah? She doesn't smell like sheep. She sits in the tent and cooks and sews. She is a real woman."

And Rachel would answer, "I like being a shepherd. I just can't change that." Then her father would stomp off, kick the dirt, and mutter strange words.

But there was one part of shepherding Rachel did not like. The well for watering the flocks had to be corked up each day with a huge rock so that all the water would not gush out and dry up. The rock was so big that every morning all the shepherds in the area had to push together to move the rock off the well. And every night they had to gather together to push it back on.

One day, on the way to morning rock pushing, Rachel saw a new man at the well. He was small and fair skinned, with warm brown eyes, and he was talking with the other shepherds at the well. Suddenly this little man, all by himself, pushed the big rock off the well. The shepherds were amazed. The man approached Rachel and said, "My name is Jacob, the son of Isaac and Rebekah. I am your cousin and I have been on a long journey. I am very happy to see you." Then Jacob kissed Rachel and started to cry because she was so very beautiful.

When the other shepherds saw Jacob crying, they said, "He is strong, but real men don't cry," and they walked away.

But Rachel did not leave Jacob. She sat by him on the rock as they watched the flocks drink from the well. Rachel said, "I never saw a man as strong as you who cries." Jacob looked at Rachel and said, "I never saw a woman as beautiful as you who is a shepherd."

They laughed and Jacob cried, and then after a time they went home—together.

The Coat of Many Colors

Brown, yellow, green, white, black, silver, red, and purple. These were the colors Joseph saw when he looked down at the beautiful new coat his father, Jacob, had just given him, and strange as it might sound, he felt the colors looking up at him.

One day Joseph dreamed a dream. He dreamed that he and his brothers were all bunches of brown wheat, and only his bunch of wheat stood up while all his brothers' bunches bowed down to him. Joseph's brothers hated him for that dream, but Joseph did not care. He was amazed that the brown color of the wheat in his dream was exactly the same color as the first brown stripe in the coat.

As if things were not bad enough, Joseph had another dream and told it to his brothers. In this dream, Joseph's brothers were stars in the sky and his father was the sun and his mother was the moon. And all of them were bowing down to Joseph. After this dream Joseph's brothers hated him so much, they left the camp to tend the flocks far away from

Joseph. Even Jacob and Rachel were not happy to hear this dream. But they loved Joseph too much to be angry at him.

And Joseph was amazed that the second stripe on the coat was the same shining yellow as the sun that had bowed down to him in his dream.

A few days later, Jacob sent Joseph to check on the flocks and make up with his brothers. Joseph finally found his brothers tending the flocks on the green hills near his home. Joseph was beginning to be afraid of the coat, because the next two stripes on the coat of many colors were green and white, just exactly the colors of the green grassy hills and the white flocks.

Joseph's brothers saw him and grabbed him, and took his coat of many colors, and threw him into a deep black pit while they decided how best to get rid of him. Without his coat in the dark blackness of the pit, Joseph could not see that the next stripe on the coat of many colors was black.

A caravan of traders on their way to Egypt was passing by just then, and the brothers decided to sell Joseph as a slave. The silver of the twenty coins flashed before Joseph's eyes as he was being pulled from the pit. And nobody even noticed the crumpled coat of many colors, whose next stripe was the same silver color as the silver coins.

When Joseph was gone, the brothers dipped the coat of many colors into the blood of a goat so that they could lie to their father and say that a wild animal had killed Joseph. They were so happy to get rid of him, they did not notice that the next stripe on the coat was red.

The brothers returned the coat of many colors with the blood all over it to their father Jacob. He fell to the ground and cried out all his tears. Then he cleaned the coat and for many days held it in his arms just like you hold a baby. He never believed the story about Joseph being killed by a wild animal—never!

Years later, a great famine hit the land of Israel. There was no food anywhere, and everyone was starving. Jacob told his sons to go down to Egypt and try to buy some food.

When they arrived in Egypt, they were brought before an Egyptian prince. He had a golden crown and a golden sword, and his robe was a deep beautiful purple, the color of the last stripe on the coat of many colors. They did not know that the Egyptian was really Joseph, their brother.

Joseph, who had done very well in Egypt, gave the brothers food, but ordered them to return with his younger brother Benjamin, whom he loved very much. When they returned to Egypt with Benjamin, the Egyptian told them that he was really their brother Joseph. The brothers were frightened at first. But Joseph told them that he was not angry with them anymore, because they had brought Benjamin safely to Egypt.

Joseph sent the brothers back to the land of Israel one more time to get the rest of the family and bring them to Egypt, where they would not starve anymore.

Jacob was very old when he saw his son Joseph again. Joseph cried and Jacob cried and the brothers cried. Even the Egyptians who were watching cried.

Then Jacob bent down and took from one of his bags the coat of many colors. The brown, yellow, green, white, black, silver, red, and purple stripes on the coat were not as bright as they once were. But they were still very beautiful.

Gently, Jacob placed the coat on the shoulders of his son Joseph. And nobody hated anybody anymore.

Moses

God needed a Jew who knew about freedom to get the people free, and Moses was the only free Jew. Really that was the main reason God picked Moses. Moses had never been a slave and had lived his whole life as a prince in the palace of the Pharaoh. There was, however, one problem with picking Moses. Moses knew that he was free, but he did not know that he was Jewish. Nobody was Jewish in the Pharaoh's palace and Moses was in the palace.

Moses' mother did her best to teach Moses that he was Jewish. After the Pharaoh's daughter found Moses floating in the Nile River, she sent for a nursemaid to take care of him when he was very little. The nursemaid turned out to be Moses' real mother. She would sing to Moses lullabies like "*Ah-ah ah-ah bubbelah, ah-ah ah-ah ketzileh.*" She would tell Moses stories about Abraham, Isaac, and Jacob and about Sarah, Rebekah, Rachel, and Leah. She would light the Shabbat candles on Friday night and make chicken soup. But Moses was just a baby then, and soon his mother was taken away.

Years later, when Moses was a grown man, he liked to take walks at night outside the palace. He would dress up like a common person and go walking among the people. One night he wandered into the neighborhood of the Jewish slaves. Moses just happened to pass by the hut of a Jewish slave family who were lighting a Shabbat lamp with the little oil they had in the house. Moses didn't understand what they were doing, but the light seemed familiar to him. He remembered the light from somewhere in his past, but he could not remember where.

The next night during his evening walk, Moses overheard a Jewish woman telling her children stories about people called Abraham, Isaac, and Jacob; Sarah, Rebekah, Rachel, and Leah. The stories sounded familiar to him, but he was not sure where he had heard them before. When the mommy was done with the stories, she sang a lullaby to her children: *"Ah-ah ah-ah bubbelah, ah-ah ah-ah ketzileh."* The song was in Moses' heart. He knew that song, but he could not remember who had first sung it to him.

On the third night, Moses tried to avoid Jews on his walk. He walked into the straw fields, but he smelled a smell that pulled him along. Following the smell, he came to the house of a Jewish slave family where the mother was making chicken soup. Moses took a deep smell and then screamed out, "MY GOD, THIS IS CHICKEN SOUP! THIS IS THE STUFF MY MOTHER MADE FOR ME WHEN I WAS A LITTLE KID! I MUST BE A JEW TOO!"

That night, back at the palace, Moses still looked like an Egyptian, but he felt like a Jew. That night, God knew everything would be all right. And so that night God lit up the burning bush and waited for Moses.

Watching
——— *the Burning Bush Burn* ———

When God set out to pick a leader for the children of Israel, the most important quality God was looking for was patience. God wanted somebody who would not give up, no matter how bad things looked, no matter how much the people complained, no matter how long it took to get to the land of Israel. God wanted a patient person to be the leader. So God set out to make a patience test that could be used to find the right person for the job.

Now the angels were always bothering God with ideas, and most of them were not very good. But God was patient, so God listened to all the angel ideas for a patience test.

Gabriel came forward with a tangled ball of string. "Whoever has the patience to untangle this ball of string is our person for sure." God did not like this test because untying knots is just boring work, and string untanglers usually are the kind of people who save rubber bands and that was not what God had in mind.

Then Michael the angel flew forward with a little puzzle box. You had to twist it so that all the red squares were on one side, and all the green on another and all the blue on another and all the yellow on another.

Michael said, "This is a great patience test! You have to figure out how to get all the same colors on all the same sides. I am still working on this one, so any person who can solve this puzzle is our person for sure."

God sent Michael away after explaining that you did not need patience to solve puzzles as much as you needed persistence. And God was convinced that some of the worst leaders had the most persistence.

Then of course God had an idea that was the very best patience test of all. God caused a bush to start burning in the desert just near where some shepherds were pasturing their flocks. A few shepherds passed it and walked away. They didn't even notice that the bush was burning, but not burning up. Bushes are not special. And bushes on fire are not that special, so nobody took the time to sit long enough to watch the miracle happen. Moses, who had run away from the palace and become a shepherd, saw the bush and sat down on the ground and watched. Moses watched and watched and saw that the bush's leaves were burned off and the bush's branches were black, just like an ordinary burning bush. The only thing different about this burning bush was that it did not burn up. It just continued to burn and burn and the branches never fell down in a heap and the fire never went out. And Moses was the only one who waited long enough to notice.

Moses tried to get the other shepherds to come over and watch the bush with him, but they all had better things to do. Moses also had better things to do, but he did not know it at the time.

The Dolphins of the Red Sea

When the children of Israel escaped from Egypt, they found the dolphins of the Red Sea waiting for them, chirping their happy dolphin chirping sounds and splashing the blue waters of the Red Sea with their flat tails.

Suddenly the people heard the terrible sounds of Pharaoh's great army chasing them from Egypt—long spears clanking, and horses' hooves pounding the dry earth as they pulled the war chariots. "We're trapped!" they cried. "If we go back to Egypt, Pharaoh and his army will kill us. And if we go forward, we will all drown in the Red Sea." But Moses raised his arm. And God zipped the Red Sea right down the middle!

The sight of the Red Sea split in half was amazing and confusing to the children of Israel. But can you imagine just how amazing and confusing this was for the *fish* of the Red Sea?

A Red Sea fish would be swimming along minding his or her own fish business when, suddenly, it would be swimming in midair—which is nowhere if you're a fish.

The dolphins tried to warn their friends the fish. They swam quickly along the edge of the walls of water, chirping a warning in fish: "Don't go there!" But the fish would ask, "What do you *mean* don't go there? Where is the *there?*" And the dolphins would answer, "There in the *air*!!" and then the fish would say, "Huh? We don't see any air there." And by that time the conversation was over because the fish were already there—in the air—which is nowhere if you're a fish.

And fish in the air was not the only problem the dolphins of the Red Sea had to face. The children of Israel left Egypt with some flocks of sheep and goats and a few cows. And on their way across the Red Sea, some of those flocks walked right through the walls of water and right into the bottom of the Red Sea—which is nowhere if you're a sheep or a goat or a cow!

So the dolphins would quickly swim down to the bottom of the Red Sea and shoo the sheep and goad the goats and carry the cows back into the air, which is somewhere if you're a cow or a sheep or a goat.

As if fish in the air and sheep in the sea were not enough to handle, the dolphins saw that the army of the Pharaoh was gaining on the children of Israel.

The dolphins tried to slow down the Pharaoh's army by flicking their tails through the walls of water and showering the wheels of the Pharaoh's war chariots so they stuck in the mud.

When the walls of water came crashing together, the children of Israel were happy because they were free at last. The fish of the Red Sea were happy because there was no air anywhere near there. The sheep and the goats and the cows were happy because there was no Red Sea anywhere near there. But most of all the dolphins of the Red Sea were happy because they could go back to doing what they liked best—chirping their dolphin chirping sounds and splashing the blue waters of the Red Sea with their flat tails.

No More Miracles!

God never liked miracles. They were too flashy, usually they hurt people, and after the miracle was over people wanted another one right away. Also the people never really believed that the miracles were coming from God. After every miracle the people would come to Moses and say, "Thanks!" and Moses would say, "Don't thank me! Thank God! God is the miracle maker; I am just the miracle bringer."

But it didn't matter what Moses said. The people thought that he was the one making the miracles. After all, they could see Moses and they could not see God. They just thought that Moses was being modest.

Moses tried everything to convince the people that it was God making the miracles. Once Moses hid under his bed before a miracle, but the people found him and said, "Moses, that was great how you did that miracle from under your bed!" Another time, when Moses knew a miracle was coming, he had someone tie him up and put a bag on his head, but after the miracle the people rushed to Moses and asked him, "How did you do the miracle all tied up like that?"

But God still gave Moses the power to do the miracles because God knew that miracles were the only thing that would convince the Pharaoh to let the children of Israel go.

The Pharaoh let the children of Israel leave Egypt, but they were stopped by the Red Sea. The people came to Moses and said, "No problem. All we need is one little miracle, Moses, and we can cross right over the Red Sea." Moses told them again that it was God and not he who was making the miracles.

Meanwhile the Pharaoh had changed his mind and was storming down on the children of Israel. Moses asked God for a very big and very quick miracle. But God said, "Sorry Moses, no more miracles."

Moses was angry. "Why did you take us out of Egypt if you were just going to let the Pharaoh kill us at the Red Sea?" So God gave Moses a very big miracle and split the Red Sea.

On the other side of the Red Sea, the children of Israel said, "Thanks Moses, that was a great miracle." And Moses said, "Don't thank me! Thank God! God is the miracle maker; I am just the miracle bringer."

Then God told Moses, "That's it! No more miracles!"

A few days later, in the desert, the children of Israel had run out of water and food and were yelling at Moses to get another miracle from God. Moses appeared before God and said, "I am really sorry to bother You again, but I don't know what You had in mind here. There are almost a million people wandering around with no water and no food."

So God sent food from the sky and water from the ground. The people said, "Thanks Moses!" and Moses said, "Don't thank me! Thank God!" And then God said, "That's it, Moses, no more miracles!"

The children of Israel needed hundreds of other miracles to get through the desert and to get into the land of Israel, and after every miracle they would say, "Thanks Moses!" and Moses would say, "Don't thank me! Thank God!" And God would say, "That's it, Moses, no more miracles!"

After Moses died many years and many miracles later, Joshua was chosen to lead the people out of the desert and into the land of Israel. Joshua also asked God to do some miracles to make getting into the land of Israel a little easier for the children of Israel. At first God said no to Joshua, but he begged God, saying, "Let me do a miracle and then the people will see that it was You all along and not Moses who made the miracles." So God gave in and did a miracle through Joshua for the people.

When it was over, the people rushed up to Joshua and said, "Great miracle, Joshua. You're just about as good a miracle maker as Moses."

Coming Home

After wandering through the desert for forty years, the children of Israel looked pretty bad. You could see the bones of the children right through their skin. And most of the cows and the sheep and the goats were so dried up, they could not give milk. At least the people did not starve to death in the desert, because of the food God sent for them, which was called "manna." Manna collected on the plants in the morning and it looked like grass seed but tasted just a little better than sand. If you mushed it up with some water and baked it, it tasted a little like bread.

Now Joshua, the servant of Moses, had been told that the land of Israel was flowing with milk and honey. Moses had told him and God had told Moses.

At night around the campfires, Joshua would tell the children of Israel stories about the land of milk and honey. When he told them about the milk and the honey, all the starving kids could think about was drinking some of that milk and eating some of that honey.

When someone would find a honeycomb in the desert, every boy and girl in the camp would line up to get a tiny piece. They would lick their fingers all day—even after the honey had been licked off—just to try and remember the taste.

On the night before entering the land of Israel, Joshua had to face the fact that he really did not know where to find the milk or where to find the honey. He was afraid to tell the children because they were so hungry.

The day the children of Israel entered the land of Israel, people were crying and singing for joy. The children ran to the river Jordan, yelling, "It's a milk river!" They dove in, swallowing huge mouthfuls of water. "Pooh!" they cried. "This river is made of water!"

Then the children of Israel saw a mountain up ahead, and they cried out, "It's a honey mountain!" They grabbed up handfuls of the mountain and stuffed it into their mouths. "Pooh!" they cried. "This mountain is made of dirt!"

That night the children of Israel camped inside the land of Israel near the river Jordan and near the mountains of Moab, where Moses had said good-bye to them. The flocks were happy and well fed on the green grass that grew near the river. The families were dancing and singing for joy. Everyone felt happy at coming home to the land that was promised to their mothers and fathers.

Joshua called together all the kids at the top of a little hill near the camp and said to them, "I want to tell you that I am sorry. I don't know where to find the milk and I don't know where to find the honey. But at least we are free and we are together. And we are home at last." Then they all looked up, and in the light of the setting sun the river looked milky white and the mountains of Moab looked honey yellow.

The next day the children found many large honeycombs in the trees near the river. And they ate and ate until nobody wanted any more. And on that day the goats and sheep and cows began to give milk again. They gave so much milk that everybody drank until they could not drink anymore.

Joshua led the people deeper into the land. But the children of the children of Israel left behind on a pile of rocks a little jar of goat's milk and a piece of honeycomb, with a note:

To God from all the kids:
Thank You for this place!

——————— *The Announcing Tool* ———————

A long time ago, when all the people lived in one place, getting the news was easy. They had yellers then who would walk around town and after a few minutes of yelling everyone got the news. But when people began living all over the place, even the yellers couldn't yell loud enough to get the news around. Mostly people just didn't get the news. But some special times just had to be announced. And the arrival of the new year was one of those times.

So God asked Enoch to go find an announcing tool.

The next day Enoch returned with two rocks. "Oh God, listen to my fine announcing tool," said Enoch, who banged the two rocks together making a loud, rock-banging sound.

God said to Enoch, "What kind of announcing tool is this to tell of the arrival of the new year? Rocks don't make music. They only make noise. The new year is a time for music and singing, not banging and yelling."

Enoch ran off to find another announcing tool.

The next day Enoch returned with a gong. "Listen to this one!" shouted Enoch as he gonged the gong, making lots of gonging sounds until God said, "STOP! What kind of announcing tool is this to announce the arrival of the new year? The gong does make a strong sound. But the gong is made of iron and iron is used to make swords and spears and arrows and other weapons of war. The new year is a time of peace, not war."

So Enoch ran off to find a new announcing tool.

The next day Enoch returned with a harp. "God, this one is a winner!" he said as he strummed some lovely harp sounds that filled the air. "Close," said God. "Very close, but not close enough. The harp is a lovely instrument. It is not noisy. It is not made of iron. But it is too soft and fine for an announcing tool. The new year is a time of loud rejoicing. We need an announcing tool that will carry the news from hilltop to hilltop around the world. Try again."

The next day Enoch returned with a golden trumpet in his hand and announced to God, "What you see here, God, is the perfect announcing tool! It makes music not noise; it is not made of iron. And it is loud enough to carry the news of the new year from hilltop to hilltop!" Enoch then blew some fine notes on the golden trumpet. Then God said, "The golden trumpet is a good announcing tool."

Enoch jumped up and down with joy until God continued, "Good, but not good enough. The golden trumpet makes loud, beautiful music and is not made of iron. But it is made by somebody who pounded it and rolled it and shaped it. I want a natural announcing tool that is not shaped by people. I want an announcing tool that is not made of gold. Prices are going up. Nobody could afford such an announcing tool." Enoch was getting depressed, but he ran off one more time to hunt down another announcing tool.

The next day Enoch was a little late in coming to God. When he did arrive, he was out of breath. "I am embarrassed, God, to show you my new announcing tool. It is only this ram's horn—not nearly as sweet as the harp or as beautiful as the golden trumpet. But it is not made of iron. And nobody pounded it or shaped it (except the ram). I even think it is loud enough to get the news from hilltop to hilltop. But I am not sure if it is a good enough announcing tool."

"Why are you not sure?" asked God.

Enoch replied, "Well, you see, Oh Holy One, Blessed be You, I have been practicing with this thing all morning and it is ever so hard to blow. Sometimes I blow and blow and all I get is a *peep!* or a *pffft!* or a *skeek!* and then maybe another *pffft!*"

God spoke to Enoch with great love: "Enoch, you have done well! The ram's horn is a perfect announcing tool. It is natural and loud and it can make beautiful sounds. I know it is hard to play, but that is just right. The new year is hard too. It is a time for deciding to do good things and give up bad things. The new year is a time for apologizing to others for hurting them in any way. And all that is very very hard to do, even harder than blowing the ram's horn."

Then God sat Enoch down and taught him to blow the ram's horn for the big celebration of the new year that was soon to begin. By the end of one lesson from God, Enoch could blow the ram's horn without a *peep!* a *pffft!* or a *skeek!*